Maverick Lesson Plans

Adaptable class activities across 10 levels of Early Readers

Contents

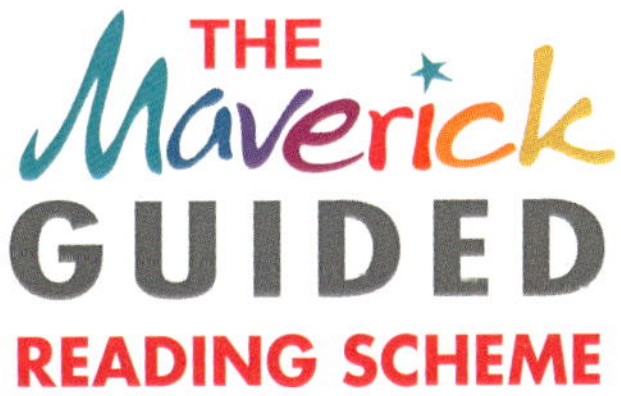

What is the Maverick Reading Scheme?

Here at Maverick, we strive to ensure all our early readers are consistent with how reading is taught in schools. Along with a team of talented authors and editors, Maverick work with top educational consultants so all our stories are ready to be used in schools from day one. We have developed our readers with a huge amount of care, making sure that each book fits the UK Institute of Education's banding criteria before they even go to publication.

How Can I Use This Book?

This guide is designed to provide teachers with simple-to-follow lesson plan ideas that can be used with any of the titles in the corresponding book band level. Lesson activities start with the Pink and Red book bands and then increase in complexity as the reading scheme develops. The activities are all designed to be very quick and easy to prepare — the majority take no more than 5 minutes!

Whilst some activities can be extended, in most cases the key idea uses little to no extra materials other than paper and pencil.

The purpose of this guide is to provide any teacher using the Maverick Early Reader story books with quick and simple ways to bring their classroom alive and make the activity of reading even more fun. The lesson plan ideas can all be used with any of the stories in the Maverick Reading Scheme, making them extremely flexible. Not only this, but as the majority of the activities are suitable for a number of different levels, you can use the same lesson plan with a different book, or a different lesson plan with the same book — the possibilities are endless!

ACTIVITY TITLE

This is an example banner of our activities. The colourful stripes represent which bands are compatible with the task.

LEVELS 1 AND 2
Pink and Red Band

Reading is quite 'new' and can potentially be stressful, so activities are designed to make the learning as fun and stress-free as possible.

ACT OUT THE STORY

Activity Details

★ Suitable levels: Pink to White

★ Materials needed: None

★ Key skills: Speaking, pronunciation, creativity

★ Estimated time to complete task: 15-20+ minutes

Note: more time will be needed as story length increases.

This activity is an easy yet entertaining way to creatively check comprehension. Split the class into small groups (depending on the number of characters in the story) and ask the strongest reader to narrate while the others act out the story.

EXTEND THE TASK!

Make face masks or finger puppets to act out the story. We have a pre-made eye mask template on our website which is great for decorating and extending — simply scan this handy QR code to find and download it for free!

MAKE A STORYBOARD

Activity Details

★ Suitable levels: Pink to White

★ Materials needed: Storyboard template (or blank paper)

★ Key skills: Creativity, presentation, speaking

★ Estimated time to complete task: 30 minutes

Only **5 MINUTES** Prep

Take a piece of paper and draw four boxes. Students can then draw the main actions of the story, and try to 'retell' it by presenting it to the class, or their group, depending on class size and level of confidence.

EXTEND THE TASK!

To develop writing skills, ask children to add speech bubbles to their storyboards. Alternatively, stronger students or higher book band levels could make a comic instead.

We have a downloadable template for this exercise, for both lower and higher levels. Simply scan this QR code to find it!

BUZZ!

Activity Details

★ Suitable levels: Pink to White

★ Materials needed: None

★ Key skills: Listening, memory

★ Estimated time to complete task: 10-15 minutes

Use this simple but fun game after reading the story to check comprehension. Choose sentences from the story but substitute one word with "buzz". Children have to shout out the missing word. This activity works well in teams if you are able to split the class into small groups. To make this harder, read out the sentence and change one word but don't say "buzz" — listeners have to instead shout out the mistake.

TOP TIP!

Make this extra fun by asking each team to create their own noise when they know the answer – animal sounds for example — or give them a noise-maker like a bell, horn or buzzer.

TOTAL PHYSICAL RESPONSE

Activity Details

- ★ Suitable levels: Pink to Orange
- ★ Materials needed: Word cards or a board
- ★ Key skills: Listening, reading
- ★ Estimated time to complete task: 15 minutes

TPR (Total Physical Response) is a great way to lift the pace and mood of the class, as well as providing a fun outlet for kinaesthetic learners. This also gets children familiar with the words before reading the story. TPR is very memorable and can be used with any number of students. It doesn't require much preparation and is a sure way to warm the children up, making them feel confident to go ahead and read the full story themselves!

TOP TIP!

Choose the words carefully: they need to be words you can easily associate with an action!

Here's what to do:

★ Choose a few words from the story and model them by doing an action at the same time as you say the word.

★ The children first copy you, and then do the action when only hearing the word.

★ The teacher now does the action only, and asks the children to shout out the word.

★ Write the word on the board or show the word card. Children now have to read it themselves and do the action.

★ Pair up learners. One does an action and the other says the word. They then swap roles until they have repeated all of the words on the board (or those on the word cards you had previously shown them).

YES OR NO GAME!

Activity Details

- ★ Suitable levels: Pink to Purple

- ★ Materials needed: None

- ★ Key skills: Listening, comprehension

- ★ Estimated time to complete task: 10-15 minutes

Check children's comprehension by making simple statements about the story — what can they remember? Explain that they must stand up if the answer is 'yes' (i.e. it's correct) and sit down if the answer is 'no' (i.e. incorrect). Model the activity with a few easy statements first, for example: "The title of the book is... Yes or no?" or "There is a dog in the story. Yes or no?"

EXTEND THE TASK!

For Green to Purple levels, why not extend the activity by splitting the class into small groups and asking each 'team' to write three new statements. They then take turns to play 'teacher' and test their classmates' memory!

RUN AND GET

Activity Details

* Suitable levels: Pink to Orange
* Materials needed: Word cards, sticky tack
* Key skills: Listening, reading
* Estimated time to complete task: 15 minutes

Make word cards with vocabulary from the story and stick them around the classroom. The word cards can be repeated, especially if the class is large. As you say a word the children have to run to the right word card and bring it back (if the class is small) or stand by it if you want to repeat the activity!

TOP TIP!

If movement is difficult, or you don't want children to get up and run around, then simply adapt the activity so they have to point in the right direction.

JIGSAW READING

Activity Details

★ Suitable levels: Pink to White

★ Materials needed: Paper that can be copied and cut into strips

★ Key skills: Reading, teamwork

★ Estimated time to complete task: 20 minutes

This is a great way to check children's comprehension, and a non-stressful way to reinforce their reading skills in an activity that is set up as a race (and therefore has a game element)!

This does require some preparation in advance, but can be done with any story, and requires no thinking time! It's really simple: copy out sentences from the story onto different strips of paper and give one 'set' to each small group. They pick up the strips of paper, one by one, so all children are included, and then have to work out together what order to put the story in.

TOP TIP!

This works really well with mixed-ability groups. As children have to work as a team, it doesn't matter if one student is weaker than the others! And if you find all groups are struggling, they can be given a copy of the book to 'check' their answer. It's not cheating if they are encouraged to reread the story — it's a win-win situation!

a plan.

dig for gold!

I love to

Pat has

Pat has a plan.

I love to dig for gold!

RHYMING CIRCLE

Activity Details

- ★  Suitable levels: Pink to White
- ★ Materials needed: Board or large piece of paper to display chosen words
- ★ Key skill: Phonics
- ★ Estimated time to complete task: 15-20 minutes

Write a few words from the story on the board and give a few rhyming and non-rhyming examples. Then organise children into small groups, standing in a circle or sat around a table. One student chooses a word from the board and they go round the circle each saying a different word that rhymes with the chosen word. If they get stuck they can choose a different word from the board and start again. Change direction every time a new starting word is chosen. The winning team is the last to finish!

TOP TIP!

It's worth taking the time to choose words you know they will be able to rhyme with plenty of others!

BINGO

Activity Details

* Suitable levels: Pink to Blue
* Materials needed: Bingo template (or blank paper), bingo counters (or pencil)
* Key skill: Listening
* Estimated time to complete task: 15 minutes

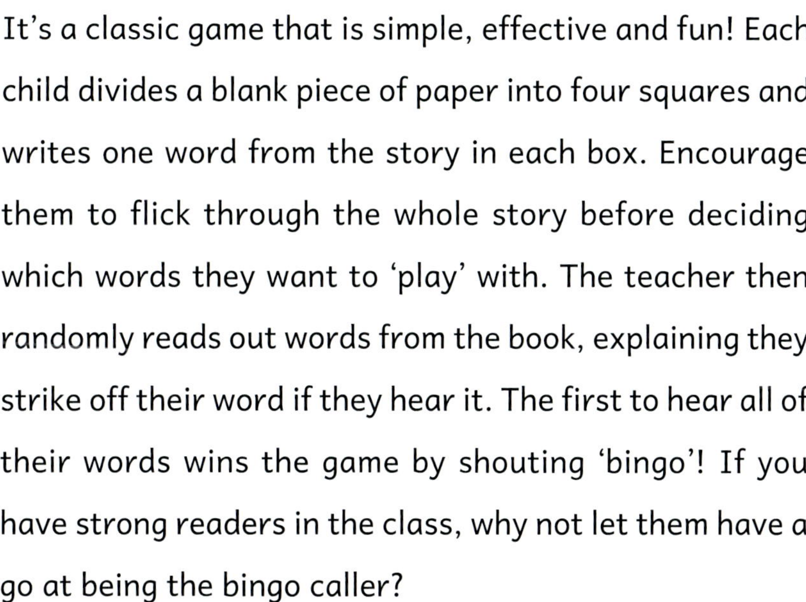

It's a classic game that is simple, effective and fun! Each child divides a blank piece of paper into four squares and writes one word from the story in each box. Encourage them to flick through the whole story before deciding which words they want to 'play' with. The teacher then randomly reads out words from the book, explaining they strike off their word if they hear it. The first to hear all of their words wins the game by shouting 'bingo'! If you have strong readers in the class, why not let them have a go at being the bingo caller?

We have a downloadable template for this exercise, for both lower and higher levels. Simply scan this QR code to find it!

LETTER CLOUDS

Activity Details

- ★ Suitable levels: Pink to Orange
- ★ Materials needed: Cloud template (or large sheets blank paper), colours
- ★ Key skills: Spelling, reading, creativity
- ★ Estimated time to complete task: 30 minutes

After reading the story, give students a letter which features in the book. This can either be chosen by you, or picked from the letter trace page that appears at the beginning of our Pink and Red stories. Ask students to find as many words as possible that use this letter in the book. Explain that the word doesn't have to start with this letter, but it needs to be included in the spelling of the word. They then, in pairs or small groups, make a letter cloud like the one on page 17. Give each group a big piece of paper on which they draw a big cloud outline. They draw the letter from the book in the middle and then decorate the cloud by drawing things that use the same letter.

We have a downloadable template for this exercise. Simply scan this QR code to find and download it!

TOP TIP!

Depending on the letter and level of the class, you might want to model this on the board and/or think of some ideas as a whole class first.

LEVELS 3 AND 4
Yellow and Blue Band

As books now consist of one longer story, you will have scope to introduce more complex activities. In addition to the next five activities, you can still use the lesson plan suggestions for the Pink and Red bands!

QUICK DRAW!

Activity Details

★ Suitable levels: Yellow to White

★ Materials needed: Word cards,
  mini-whiteboards (or blank paper)

★ Key skills: Creativity, memory

★ Estimated time to complete task: 20 minutes

Select words from the story and write each one on a word card. Make enough copies for each group. Place the pile of word cards face down in the middle of each group's table. Students take turns to pick up a word card for which they must draw until their team can guess the word on the card. The winning team is the group who gets through all the words the fastest in this entertaining version of Pictionary™.

TOP TIP!

Choose the words based on what you think your class will be able to draw!

MAKE YOUR OWN WORDSEARCH

Activity Details

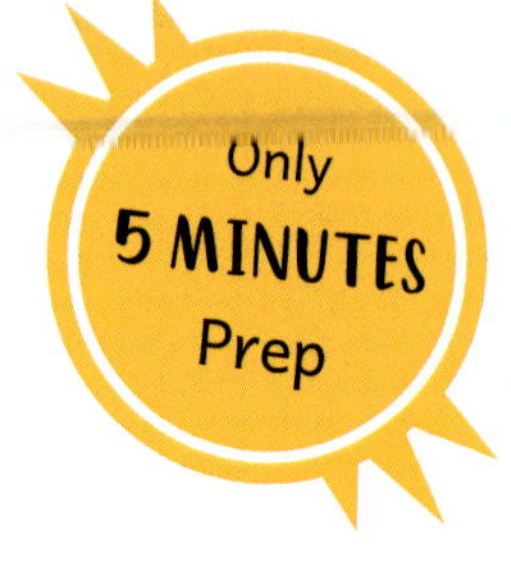

* Suitable levels: Yellow to White

* Materials needed: Wordsearch template (or grid paper)

* Key skills: Spelling, writing

* Estimated time to complete task: 30 minutes

This is a fantastic, student-led activity to get children more familiar with letters and spelling. It focuses on their writing skills in a very basic, controlled way.

Give each child a wordsearch template or grid paper and ask them to choose 8 words from the story. They should write the list of words on the paper so that it is clear which words are to be found later! Next explain that they need to complete the wordsearch grid, first with the selected words, and then by filling in all of the remaining squares with random letters.

Make it clear (depending on the children's level) whether they should use horizontal (left to right) and vertical (top to bottom) words only, or if they can make it more challenging by including diagonals or words written in reverse. Once completed, they swap with another child and try to find their partner's words before they find theirs!

TOP TIP! We have a downloadable template for this exercise, for both lower and higher levels. Simply scan this QR code to find it! Also, many of the activity packs available to download on our website include a ready-made wordsearch with words from the story. See page 48 for more information.

ALPHABET RACE

Activity Details

* Suitable levels: Yellow to Purple

* Materials needed: Word cards

* Key skills: Reading, spelling, teamwork

* Estimated time to complete task: 15 minutes

Take key vocabulary from the story and write each word on a word card. To lower preparation time, write words on one sheet and photocopy/print before cutting up!

Make enough copies to complete the activity in small groups, i.e. for a class of 30 you might want 10 copies so they can play in groups of 3. The children 'race' to be the fastest team to put the word cards in alphabetical order.

EXTEND THE TASK!

For higher levels, choose words that begin with the same first letter but different second or third letter — this makes the task much more difficult!

DON'T SAY IT!

Activity Details

★ Suitable levels: Yellow to White

★ Materials needed: Word cards

★ Key skill: Speaking

★ Estimated time to complete task: 20 minutes

This is a fun activity based on the popular Taboo™ game. Make word cards with vocabulary from the story and include words that they cannot use in the description. An example would be:

BEAR **Can't say:** Animal, Teddy or Goldilocks

The objective is to get the class (or your team) to say the word (without using the 'can't say' words). Take turns so everyone has the chance to give a description. Assign time limits or a points system as you see fit!

TOP TIP!

Divide bigger classes into groups so as to include as much student participation as possible — you'll therefore need a set of cards for each group!

FIVE SENSES WHEEL

Activity Details

★ Suitable levels: Yellow to White

★ Materials needed: Wheel template (or blank paper), colours

★ Key skills: Sensory engagement, imagination

★ Estimated time to complete task: 30 minutes

Use this activity to get children thinking about the five senses. Draw a large circle on a piece of paper and divide it into five segments. Once you have the 'spokes' of the wheel, make a small inner circle and draw the relevant body parts: eyes, ears, nose, mouth, hands. Then, on the outer rim you write: "I can see..", "I can hear..." and so on, in the relevant section, and students complete the wheel from the perspective of the story. They can include words or pictures, or a combination of both!

We have a downloadable template for this exercise. Simply scan this QR code to find and download it!

EXTEND THE TASK!

For speaking practice, you could ask the children to present their wheel to the class or group.

LEVELS 5 AND 6

Green and Orange Band

Adding to the previous lesson plan ideas, we can now introduce activities to complement the progression of the reading scheme. Children will be given the opportunity to practise more complex spelling for example.

Activity Details

★ Suitable levels: Green to White

★ Materials needed: Blank paper

★ Key skill: Spelling

★ Estimated time to complete task: 25 minutes

This is a simple but fun game to practise spelling. Draw a shape on the board, in which you randomly put the letters of a word from the story, for example:

Ask the children if they can remember a word from the story that uses each of these letters once (the answer in this case would be 'friend'!). Once you've given a few examples, put children in pairs and ask them to choose different words from the story and create their own anagram shapes on a piece of paper. They then swap with their partner and see who can guess the words first.

TIMELINE

Activity Details

★ Suitable levels: Green to White

★ Materials needed: Timeline template (or blank paper)

★ Key skills: Writing, memory, imagination

★ Estimated time to complete task: 30 minutes

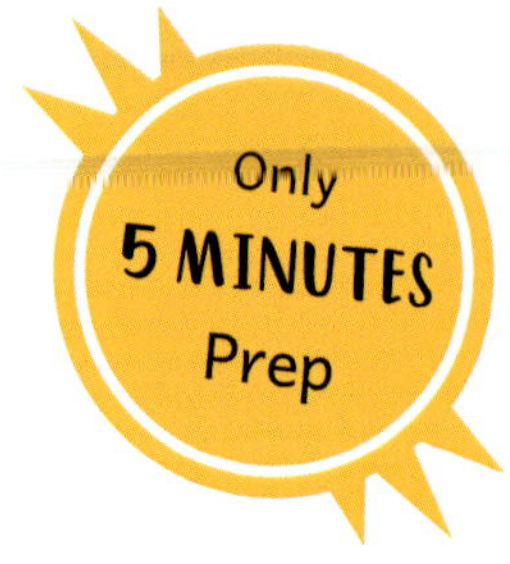

This is a great way to check children's comprehension. Whilst testing their memory of the storyline, they should also be encouraged to use their imagination as they will need to invent logical dates and/or times and perhaps want to add in extra details! Hand out a template timeline to each child (or draw an example on the board) and ask them to complete it with as many different events as possible.

We have a downloadable template for this exercise. Simply scan this QR code to find and download it!

SYLLABLE SORTING, 1, 2, 3!

Activity Details

★ Suitable levels: Green to White

★ Materials needed: Word cards

★ Key skill: Phonemes

★ Estimated time to complete task: 25 minutes

1. Teach the concept of a syllable by reading some of the story and clapping each syllable. Include examples of 1, 2 and 3 syllables words. Ask children to listen, repeat, and clap along.

2. Hand out word cards (all 1, 2 or 3-syllable words) to each small group and ask the children to put them in three piles according to the number of syllables.

3. Finish with a game! Ask children to shuffle the word cards and place them face down. Each child picks up a card and reads the first syllable only. If it's a one-syllable word, they win the card. If it has more than one syllable, the first child to complete the word wins the card. Whoever has the most cards wins!

ALPHABET POSTERS

Activity Details

* Suitable levels: Green to White
* Materials needed: Large pieces of paper, colours
* Key skills: Reading, spelling, creativity
* Estimated time to complete task: 40 minutes

By these levels, the stories are longer and contain a wider range of vocabulary. For a fun activity get your students to design an alphabet poster, and illustrate each letter with a word they find in the story. Encourage children's creativity, but if they can't draw something then they can write the word itself. Tell them not to worry if they can't find an example for all 26 — there won't be a word beginning with X (and some others, depending on the story) but they can just colour the letter itself.

EVERYTHING WE KNOW ABOUT...

Activity Details

★ Suitable levels: Orange to White

★ Materials needed: Large pieces of paper, colours

★ Key skills: Research, teamwork

★ Estimated time to complete task: 50 minutes

This activity can be used to feed children's interest in things they have read about in the story. After reading the book each small group will choose a research topic (an animal or object from the story for instance) and do a short project to present to the class.

Depending on the skills and interests of your class you could choose any of the project ideas below or, even better, give them the choice!

NO Preparation Needed

PROJECT IDEAS!

Ask the children to write a script for a TV documentary, create a poster, make an information pamphlet, or write a poem.

LEVELS 7 AND 8

Turquoise and Purple Band

Stories have continued to increase in length and now offer a great opportunity for the reader to get involved in more complex tasks. All activities still focus on fun!

SUPER SURVEYS

Activity Details

* Suitable levels: Turquoise to White
* Materials needed: Grid (or blank) paper and pencil
* Key skills: Speaking, statistics
* Estimated time to complete task: 40 minutes

This is a fantastic student-led activity that not only gets children talking, but also integrates basic maths (statistics) skills. Ask children to write one question about the book, and explain that they are going to interview the rest of the class to find out their answers. Make it clear that they will have to write down the possible answers, and then count up the final number of responses to each. They can then be shown how to plot the results on a bar chart, which can be displayed around the class.

CHARACTER LIFELINE

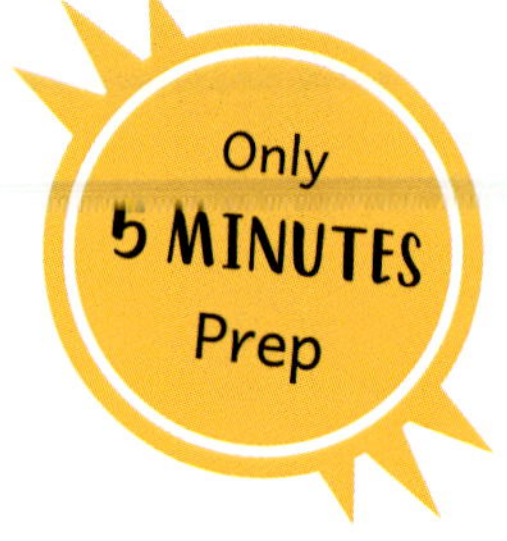

Activity Details

* Suitable levels. Turquoise to White
* Materials needed: Lifeline template or blank paper
* Key skills: Imagination, writing, creativity
* Estimated time to complete task: 40 minutes

Ask children to choose a character from the story and imagine how their life changes as they get older. Give them a template, or model an example on the board, and ask them to fill in each stage with a point in their life, for example: baby, child, teenager, adult, old person. Explain to the children that they can choose how to depict each life stage. It could be a drawing, a written description, or a combination of the two, making it well suited to mixed-ability classes.

We have a downloadable template for this exercise. Simply scan this QR code to find and download it!

MAKE YOUR OWN QUIZ

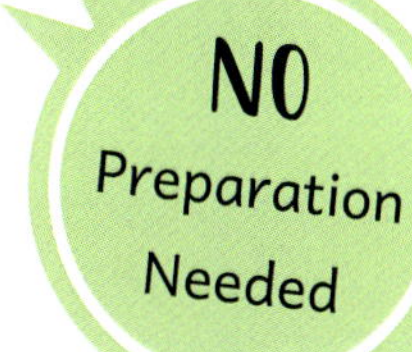

Activity Details

* Suitable levels: Turquoise to White
* Materials needed: Pen and paper
* Key skills: Reading, writing
* Estimated time to complete task: 30 minutes

Divide the class into small groups and give them a realistic target, e.g. groups of three to come up with five different questions about the story. They may need help in writing the question, but the focus should be on the development of the ideas and the use of the language in a very natural way. The quiz will be 'played' orally, so you needn't worry about spelling mistakes — as long as the group remembers their question (and the correct answer!) then the written work should be secondary.

EXTEND THE TASK!

For stronger classes, why not focus more on correct grammar and spelling? Ask groups to come up with a few more questions and write out a quiz sheet to be swapped between teams.

WHAT HAPPENS NEXT?

Activity Details

★ Suitable levels: Turquoise to White

★ Materials needed: Pen and paper

★ Key skills: Imagination, writing

★ Estimated time to complete task: 45 minutes

This is a great way to give readers the opportunity to really use their imagination. Put children into small groups, ideally with three children, and explain that they are going to come up with a sequel to the story. They should be encouraged to work orally first, to discuss ideas, and then agree on the beginning, middle and end of their story. Each group member then writes one part (which is why teams of three is ideal!) — beginning, middle or end. Stories can then, time permitting, be read out to the class.

EXTEND THE TASK!

Why not ask groups to act out their story? Or get arty and make a comic!

SINGER-SONGWRITER!

Activity Details

* Suitable levels: Turquoise to White

* Materials needed: None (see top tip!)

* Key skills: Creativity, rhythm

* Estimated time to complete task: 40 minutes

The idea of this musical task is to create a song about the story. It works best if children can listen to an example first. Choose a well-known song and prepare a few lines yourself. Creativity is key — the lyrics can be taken directly from the book, but make it clear that they can invent the lyrics as well! Get them to sing along to your song first — try 'Happy Birthday' or a song you are sure everyone will know. Then put children into small groups and ask them to do the same with a melody of their choice.

TOP TIP!

Children will love this activity even more if you can give them some percussion instruments. Tambourines, rattles, triangles, anything that makes noise! This also aids shy children if you ask them to perform their song to the class.

LEVELS 9 AND 10
Gold and White Band

The previous activities will still make a fun addition to any class, however the scope for extending the activities outside the comprehension of the story itself is much greater. Children will enjoy putting their creative writing skills to the test with more independent tasks.

BOOK REVIEW

Activity Details

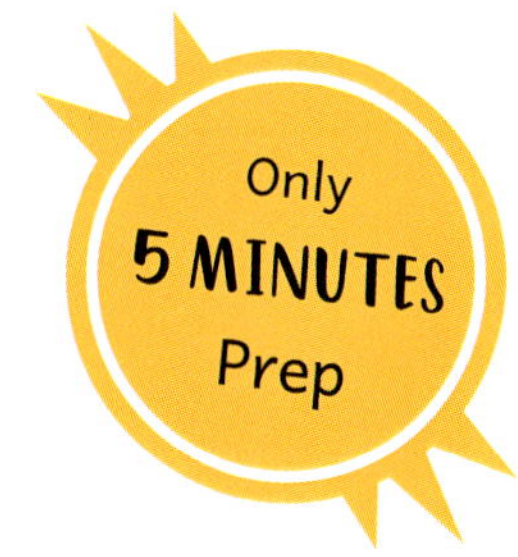

* Suitable levels: Gold to White
* Materials needed: Pen and paper
* Key skill: Writing
* Estimated time to complete task: 50 minutes

After reading the book, ask children to discuss their opinion of the story. Divide the class into small groups and give them some questions on the board in order to help guide them. Do this orally first as it will help them to generate ideas. Next, ask children to write down their opinions, to form a book review. They can then swap and read each others, and perhaps decide if their reviews were the same, similar, or different!

EXAMPLE QUESTIONS!

Did you like the story? What was your favourite part? Was there anything you didn't like? Who was the most interesting character and why? Who would you recommend this book to? How many stars would you give the book?

CHAPTER QUIZ

Activity Details

★ Suitable levels: Gold to White

★ Materials needed: Pen and paper

★ Key skills: Writing, memory

★ Estimated time to complete task: 30 minutes

Books at these levels are now divided into short chapters as stories are longer. Why not get the students to create a chapter quiz as a quick but fun way to check their memory?

Split students into pairs or groups, and model an example question on the board: "In which chapter did Freddie's class visit the museum?". Ask children to write five questions, then swap 'quiz sheets' between groups.

EXTEND THE TASK!

For larger classes, ask children to write their answers on a separate paper so that the quiz sheets they create can be circulated to different pairs/groups in the class.

DIARY ENTRIES

Activity Details

★ Suitable levels: Gold to White

★ Materials needed: Pen and paper

★ Key skills: Writing, imagination

★ Estimated time to complete task: 30 minutes

This activity really develops both the child's imagination and writing skills. Ask them to choose a character from the book and write a diary entry for a week.

TOP TIP!

This activity is perfect for mixed-ability classes — those who struggle with writing can be encouraged by just using note-form diary entries whereas stronger students have the space to write longer, more complex sentences.

We have a downloadable template for this exercise. Simply scan this QR code to find and download it!

PUT YOURSELF IN THE STORY!

Activity Details

★ Suitable levels: Gold to White

★ Materials needed: None

★ Key skills: Imagination, creativity

★ Estimated time to complete task: 30 minutes

This activity works well for groups with a lot of imagination! Make sure they have read the story twice, and have a good understanding of the storyline. Ask them to imagine that they are a new character in the book! Give them some time to think individually, and then ask them to talk in small groups to tell their classmates how they fit into the story.

EXTEND THE TASK!

Group students together and ask them to act out a new version of the story, using their own new characters — they will be acting, but playing themselves!

WHO SAID IT?

Activity Details

★ Suitable levels: Gold to White

★ Materials needed: Pen and paper

★ Key skill: Memory

★ Estimated time to complete task: 30 minutes

This activity, whilst following a very simple concept, will test children's memory skills quite well! Make sure your story has plenty of direct speech. Put children into small groups and ask them to write five questions, which they will later ask to a different team. You will need to model this on the board so they are clear about what to do. Here is an example:

INDEX

All starred activities require
5 minutes or less preparation.

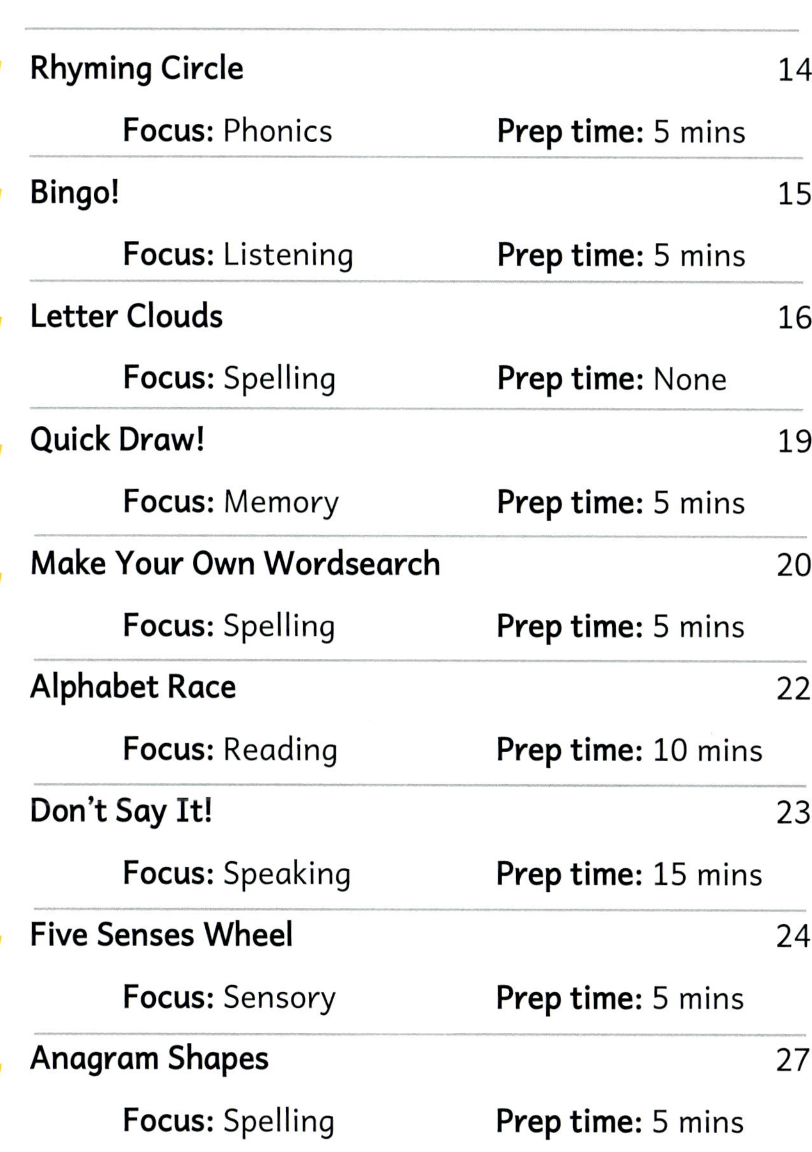

INDEX

ONLINE RESOURCES

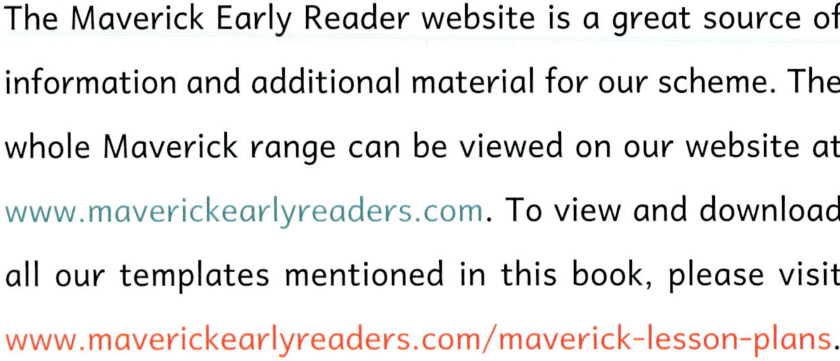

The Maverick Early Reader website is a great source of information and additional material for our scheme. The whole Maverick range can be viewed on our website at www.maverickearlyreaders.com. To view and download all our templates mentioned in this book, please visit www.maverickearlyreaders.com/maverick-lesson-plans.

Activity Packs

Our activity packs can be used instantly and are a great resource for children who have read any of our books, with varying exercises depending on the band. All of our activity packs are free to download, print and distribute!

Audio

Our early readers come with audio support with reading-along features. Videos for most of our Pink to Blue Band titles can be viewed in the classroom. The audio files for all titles from Pink to White can be downloaded for free.

Want to see our website right now?
Simply scan this QR code to view it!